TOP SECRET!

With thanks to Tia, Mia, Isobel, Alex, Capri, Samilla, Eloise and Grace for their excellent ideas—M.C.

For our drama besties, Hannah and Elvie—D.M.

Scholastic Australia
An imprint of Scholastic Australia Pty Limited
PO Box 579 Gosford NSW 2250
ABN 11 000 614 577
www.scholastic.com.au

Part of the Scholastic Group
Sydney • Auckland • New York • Toronto • London • Mexico City • New Delhi • Hong Kong • Buenos Aires • Puerto Rico

Published by Scholastic Australia in 2021.

NATIONAL LIBRARY OF AUSTRALIA
A catalogue record for this book is available from the National Library of Australia

ISBN: 978-93-5471-604-1

Typeset in Sweetie Pie.

This reprint edition: December 2023
Printed in India at Ram Printograph Delhi

ELLA Diaries

Diva DRAMA

Sunday night

Dear Diary,

The most aMAZing thing happened today!

I was sitting quietly in my bedroom working on my latest Animal Fact File. (It was all about slow lorises in case you were wondering.)

And there was a KNOCK on my door.

I didn't answer it because it was probably just Olivia, my annoying little sister.

Olivia is *always* coming into my room and doing exTREMEly annoying and irritating things, like:

taking stuff off my shelves and putting it back in the wrong place,

or borrowing my BEST coloured markers and never, ever, EVER (to the power of 100) returning them,

or lying on my bed . . . WITH HER ROLLERSKATES ON!!! ⊙

And then there was *another* knock. A bit louderer this time.

I was just starting to call out, 'Go away, Olivia, I'm busy,' when the door opened.

And guess who was standing there?

If you said Olivia you are wrong, wrong, **WRONG**.

It was Mum.

Looking at me with exCEPTionally shiny eyes. So shiny I could see all my fluffy bed toys reflected in them.

And guess why her eyes were all shiny?

You never will, so I'll just tell you.

Mum does designering work for a big importerant advertising company. And they **DESPERATINGLY** need two girls to be in one of their ads.

On TV!!!

And Mum said she told them she knows someone who would be **PERFECT** for it.

And guess who that someone is?

HINT: It rhymes with something that has salty water and wavy waves.

And guess what else? The advertising people said yes! Straightaway right then IMMEDIATELY!

(Mainly because the two girls (who are real actorers from a real actoring place) who were supposed to be doing the ad suddenly couldn't.)

And all the filming for it will be in the school holidays. Which are **NEXT WEEK!**

Being in an ad on TV is PERFECT for me.

REASONS WHY BEING IN A TV AD IS PERFECT FOR ME

1. I ♥ watching TV. Even the ads!

2 I am exCEPTionally good at actoring. (And also singing. And dancing. And doing gymnastics. And directoring. But **mainly** actoring.)

3 Being on TV has always been one of my **Top Three** main ambitions. (After saving the planet and inventing a new colour.)

And guess what else?

They want me to bring along a friend. So I'm going to ask Zoe!

Zoe is my BFFFE*. We do (mostly) everything together.

* BFFFE = Best Friend Forever For Ever

I was **DYING** to race straight around to her place so I could tell her all about my amazing news.

But Mum said I couldn't, because Nanna Kate was coming to our place for dinner. And then after that we were all going to have a lovely time looking at her Antarctica trip photos.

So I'll just have to wait until I see her at school tomorrow.

Good night!

Love,

Ella

Monday, after school

Dear Diary,

I waited on the corner where Zoe and I always meet up every morning so we can walk to school together.

And waited . . .

And waited . . .

And waited . . .

Until I couldn't wait **ANY LONGER**, or I would have been late for school. So I ran the whole rest of the way.

But Zoe wasn't in the playground.

Or the line waiting to go into our classroom.

I even checked under our table, in case she was hiding from me.

But she wasn't. ☹

It was **SO NOT FAIR**, Diary. I was desperatingly desperate to find Zoe so I could tell her all about us being specially chosen to be on TV.

And she hadn't even bothered coming to school. ☹

And then I saw something out of the far corner of my eye.

A little face at the window, peering into our classroom.

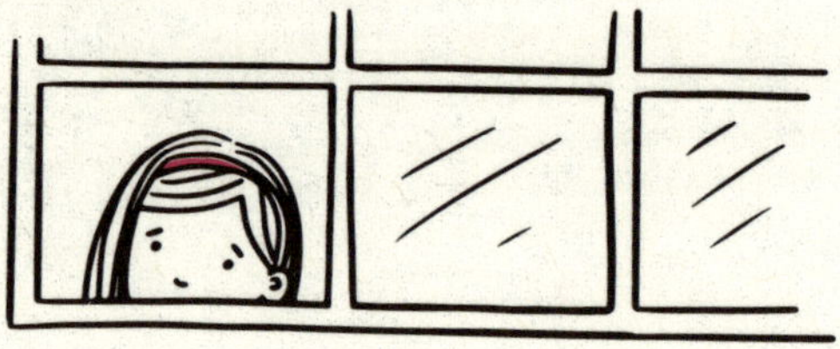

And a little hand, knocking on our door.

It was Zoe's hand. (And also her face.) YES!!!
I could finally tell her!

Except Ms Weiss told Zoe to come inside and sit down quietly and get on with her work. So I STILL couldn't tell her my news, even though it was bubbling inside of me trying to get out, just like boiling red-hot lava bubbling inside a red-hot dangerous volcano.

So I had to wait until

Sorry, Diary. I have to stop writing now. Max is being **SUPER** loud and annoying. So Mum wants me to read him a story to calm him down while she finishes off some importerant designering work.

I'll be back soon. Promise!

E

About fifteen minutes later . . .

I'm back!

So anyway, as soon as the bell rang for recess Zoe and I ran out into the playground.

By now I was **BUSTING** to tell Zoe my special news.

~~Unforch~~ Unfortunately, Zoe was EVEN MORE BUSTING to go somewhere else. So I went with her.

All the cubicles were full! So we had to wait in front of the wash basins. Here's what we said while we were waiting.

Me (exciteredly): I have some super-excitering and fantabulous news to tell you!

Zoe (puzzled): Don't you want to know why I was late to school?

Me: Why were you late to school?

Zoe (tapping her teeth): Dentist appointment. I had a toothache.

Me: Oh yeah. I forgot.

Zoe: So, what's your super-exciting news?

Me (grinning): Guess.

Zoe: Our school is closing down and turning into a horse-riding school instead?

Me: Nope. Guess again.

Zoe: Our class is going on an excursion to a giganterous chocolate factory?

Me: Nope. Guess again.

Zoe: An internationally famous movie director wants to make a movie about our lives? And we're going to be the stars of it?

Me: No. But close. Mum—

And then all the cubicle doors opened up at once and the girls inside them came **rushing out** into the handwashing part.

I stopped telling Zoe the super-excitering news because we could **finally** go into our own cubicles.

By the time we came back out everyone was gone. Vanished. Vamoosed*.

* Vamoosed is a word Nanna Kate (and also Mum) uses sometimes. Dad thinks she made it up, but it is a real live word. It means 'to leave a place in a hurry'. It does NOT mean you leave that place on a moose. That would just be weird.

So I told her all about how I had been chosen by an importerant advertising company to be in an importerant ad. On TV. And how they wanted me to bring a friend along, to be in the importerant ad with me.

Zoe *also* looked at me with shiny eyes. So shiny I could see the shiny soap dispenserers on the wash basins reflected in them.

And then she asked me if I knew who the friend was going to be.

And I said I hadn't **TOTALLY** 100 per cent made up my mind yet, but I had a *fairly* good idea. ☺

We were just about to leave when I noticed something out of the far corner of my eye.

The door of the cubicle right at the end was closed. Which meant . . .

Da da da . . . DUMMMMMM.

Somebody was in there.

And then we both ran outside into the sunny sunshine.

Sorry, but I have to stop writing AGAIN, Diary. Zoe is coming over VERY SOON for an ETVAM (Emergency TV Ad Meeting).

And I need to get everything organised for it! (Including the snacks and the KEEP OUT sign for my door.)

Yours truly,
Ella

Monday night, in bed

Dearest Diary,

Zoe and I had our ETVAM!

The first thing we did was eat all the snacks.

I FOUND THESE IN THE CUPBOARD. THEY WERE PERFECT FOR OUR meeting!

Then Zoe got out the list of questions for me that she had (secretly) put together while we were working on our Life on the Goldfields projects this afternoon.

The first question was:

1. What is the importerant TV ad about?

OOPS!

I had ~~absolootly~~ ~~absolewtly~~ absolutely NO IDEA! Not even a teensy tiny one!

That's because I'D FORGOTTEN TO ASK MUM!

So Zoe and I stopped having our ETVAM and ran down the hallway and into Mum's study instead.

And guess what she told us the ad was about?

EGGS!

Bleuchhhh!

I don't even *like* eggs!

Why couldn't it have been another type of healthy food? Like bananas? I ♥ bananas, especially when they are in banana splits.

YUM!

Or mangoes! Mangoes are YUM!

We could even do a Mango Tango! Wearing those stylishly stylish long frilly dresses tango-dancing ladies wear!

But Mum said we probably didn't have to actually *EAT* the eggs. (Eggs. Eww.)

We just had to do stuff like bounce around on a trampoline and look happy and carefree while we said nice things about eggs.

Like how healthy and good and fantabulously fabulous they are for you.

PHEWWW!

Zoe didn't even have any more questions for me after that. So we went out into the backyard and practised our walks for when we are BIG TV STARS instead.

Good night!

Love,

Ella

XX

PS **I CANNOT BELIEVE** I forgot to write this next part earlier. Precious Princess Peach Parker asked me if I wanted to come shopping for a new outfit with her and her mum after school today.

Which is just **WEIRD**. Princess Peach **NEVER** asks me to do stuff like that.

When I asked her why she wanted me to come she said, 'No reason. You just have an exCEPtionally good sense of STYLE.'

Tuesday, after dinner

Dear Diary,

I was just running out the door this morning to go to school when Mum handed me a piece of paper.

And guess what it was?

An email message from the TV ad people! With some of the lines* I have to learn for my part in the ad!

* 'Lines' is the special name for the words an actorer says when they are in a play or a movie or an ad on TV.

At lunchtime, Zoe and I (and also Ammy) slipped away to our special part of the playground, making extra sure nobody followed us.

We don't want any of our friends to know what we're doing yet. That would spoil the **BIG SURPRISE** when they see us on TV! ☺

I unfolded the piece of paper Mum gave me, and read some of the lines out loud to Zoe and Ammy.

Then we all had a practice saying them.

(Including Ammy, in case Zoe or I got eggs-tremely sick with lumperous throats and itcherous red rashes on the filming day, and we needed an EEE*.)

* EEE = Emergency Egg Eggs-pert.

Here are some of the lines we said.

We all sounded amazing! And egg-cellent! And fantabulously fabulous!

I was just telling Zoe and Ammy that the TV ad people also wanted us to do some egg flips* while we bounce on the trampoline when . . .

DOOT! DOOT! DOOT!

. . . the bell for the end of lunchtime dooted.

* Egg flips are like backflips, only we have to hold an egg while we're doing them.

NORMAL ORDINARY FLIP

EGG FLIP

'Egg flip' is also the name for a fancy vanilla milkshake with eggs in it (eww) that Nanna Kate likes to drink.

So we all ran back to our classroom to line up outside. Zoe couldn't stop talking about the ad! She's going to come to my place **tomorrow after school** so we can practise our lines a bit more. I asked Ammy if she wanted to come too, but she's got soccer practice. So she can't.

Zoe and I were just having another little chat about the egg flips when someone tapped me on the shoulder.

And guess who it was?

See what I mean about Peach acting really **weird** all of a sudden?

Princess Peach usually only ever talks about how amazing and fabulous her own perfect hair looks.

But the way she said 'egg-cellent' sounded just like one of the lines from our TV ad. Wait . . . Peach couldn't **possibly** know about that.

COULD SHE???

No way. I probably just didn't hear what she said properly.

Later on, Peach asked me if I wanted to borrow one of her special brand-new glittery Glitterama pens, so I could colour in a picture for my Life on the Goldfields project.

I have been DESPERATINGLY DYING to try out one of those Glitterama pens, ever since I saw them in an ad on TV.

So I did.

It was aMAZing! And GLITTERy! And FANTABulously FABulous!

I'm going to ask Peach if I can try the silver one tomorrow!

Bye for now!
Ella
x

Wednesday night, in bed, very, very late

Dearest Diary,

You will never, ever, EVER guess what happened today.

Not even if you had a guess for every single second of the next million, pazillion, PATRILLION years.

So I might as well just tell you.

When I came back into class after recess this morning, there was a **sweet little envelope** nestled between the pages of my Maths book.

It was from Peach!

Peach **NEVER** leaves me little notes.

FOR ELLA
FROM PEACH

I showed the envelope to Zoe.

So I did. And guess what it said?

Dear Ella

Can you please come over to my house after school today?

It is super super SUPER important.

Yours truly

Peach

xxx

I was shocked!

But also ~~intreeged~~ ~~intrieged~~ intrigued*. Peach **NEVER** invites me to come to her place.

* 'Intrigued' means when you are really, really curious about something. So curious you HAVE to find out straightaway right now or you will **burst** into smithereens.

Zoe wasn't intrigued though. She was worried about me.

And so was Ammy, when we told her about Peach's letter.

And then they BOTH reminded me that Zoe was coming over to my place after school so we could practise our lines.

So I wouldn't be able to go to Peach's place anyway.

But then they said something else.

A trick! Maybe. Peach **DOES** play tricks on people. And sometimes she can be a bit mean. ☹

But maybe Zoe and Ammy are just saying that because I got a letter and they didn't?

I really, really, **REALLY** wanted to know what Peach thought was so **SUPER IMPORTANT**. But I also didn't want to hurt Zoe's feelings.

So I made a plan to go to Peach's place without Zoe (or Ammy) finding out.*

* I told Mum of course. Mum always knows **EVERYTHING**. ☺

Here's my plan.

ELLA'S EXCELLENT PLAN

STEP 1

walk home from school with Zoe like I do every day.

STEP 2

Convince Zoe (kindly) she can't come inside to practise our lines by telling her my little brother Max has an

exTREMEly lumperous throat and itcherous red rash. (Eww.) And is also exTREMEly ~~contayjus~~ contagious, so NO VISITORS ALLOWED.

STEP 3

Ask Mum if I can go to Peach's house for a quick visit.

STEP 4

Say 'Yes, totally,' when Mum says, 'Peach's house?'

Step 5

Ask Mum (or Dad, if Mum is too busy) to drive me to Peach's house, to avoid being seen out on the street.

Step 6

Sneak out of our house in disguise and jump in and out of our car quickly in case Zoe or Ammy happen to be walking past at EXACTLY the same time.

And guess what? My plan worked!

I managed to get all the way to Peach's front door without anyone recognising me!

Even Peach! ☺

The first thing we did was have some stylish snacks by her pool.

Then we came back inside and went up some stairs to her brand-new bedroom and play area. She even has her **OWN BATHROOM**. With a **BATH** in it!

Peach told me I am the very first person out of **ALL** of her pazillions of friends to see her new room. And she wants me to help her choose the colours for her new matching curtains and bedspread.

Me!!!

Here are some of the different designs she showed me.

Then after that we drew stylish portraits of each other.

Peach has the **biggest** and the **best** stationery collection I have ever seen in my **WHOLE ENTIRE LIFE.**

And guess what? She said I can borrow any of her glitter pens or pencils or coloured fabric paints **WHENEVER I WANT!** ♥

And guess what else?

I was casually looking out of the window while I was washing my hands in her new (exceptionally stylish) bathroom when I saw something down on the lawn below.

So I raced back out again.

ZOW-IE. Peach is soooo lucky. If I had my own trampoline, I could practise egg flips for our TV ad on it all day long.

I asked Peach if she knew how to do backflips. And she said, 'Of course!'

And then she said I should come over again soon and we could do some different kinds of flips together.

That sounds like funnerous fun!

I hope it happens soon.

Bye for now.

Yours,

Ella

XOXOXO

Thursday afternoon, straight after school

Dear Diary,

Something **horrendously horrible** happened today.

So horrendously horrible I'm not 100 per cent sure what I'm going to do. ☹

I was waiting for Zoe on our corner like we do every morning so we can walk to school together. And Zoe walked **straight** past me, with her head in the air. Just like she was in a **big snit** with me.

So I called out to her. **Twice.**

But Zoe didn't turn around. She just kept right on walking. Super super fast. And she kept on walking like that the whole way to school.

And then when we got to school she didn't talk to me. Not even when I accidentally-on-purpose stood on her foot when we were lining up to go into class.

Or at recess.

Or when I desperatingly needed a partner to go to the toilet with me.

So I had to ask Fiona MacTavish to be my toilet partner instead. ☹

Zoe *still* wasn't talking to me at lunchtime.

So as soon as Zoe left to get a drink from the bubblers, I asked Ammy if she knew why.

And Ammy said it was because Zoe found out that I'd gone to Peach's house after school yesterday.

And she was **SUPER** upset about it. **EsPECially** because I had told her a big fib about Max.

Ammy said Zoe knew I was fibbing after she saw Max playing soccer in the park with Dad on her way home.

And he didn't look sick (or even contagious).
Not even ONE LITTLE BIT.

OOPS.

And then Ammy told me something even ~~badderer~~ ~~worserer~~ worse.

Poppy was driving past Peach's house with her mum. And she saw me:

1. climbing out of my car and sneaking up to Peach's front doorstep,

2. knocking on her door,

3. and going inside.

Which is really **weird**, Diary, because I was wearing my cunning disguise the

WHOLE TIME.

DOUBLE OOPS.

Then Poppy told Daisy.

And Daisy told Georgia.

And Georgia told Chloe.

And then Chloe told Zoe.

And now my BFFFE is **super** mad at me. And she probably isn't ever going to talk to me **ever** again.

And it's **ALL MY FAULT**.

Ella ☹

Thursday afternoon, a bit later

Dear Diary,

I can't believe what just happened.

I was sitting on my bed, trying to learn my lines for our importerant TV ad and worrying about Zoe.

And then Olivia barged in.

WITHOUT EVEN KNOCKING FIRST. ☹

She started messing about with all the stuff on my dressing table, opening things up and moving them around.

So I told her to get out of my room **RIGHT NOW**.

And then after she'd gone out I slammed the door really, really loudly. Like this.

And then Olivia had a big tanty, and started calling out for Mum.

And then about ninety-six seconds after that Mum came into my room and sat down on my bed next to me.

So then everything came flooding out of me like flooding water gushing down a giganterous drain.

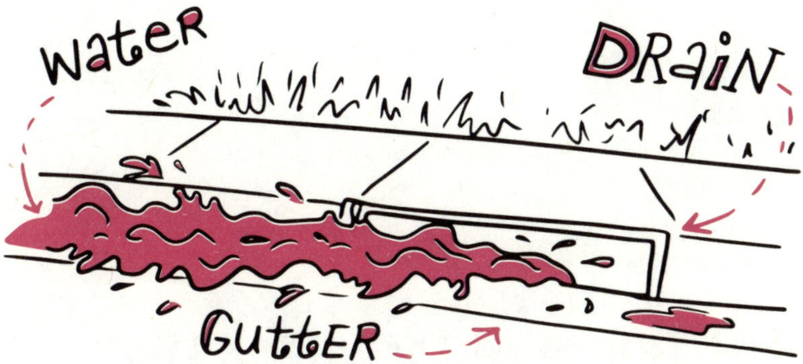

I told Mum all about how I'd been mean to Zoe. And that she was never going to speak to me ever again.

And Mum said maybe I should call her on the phone to say sorry.

But I was too worried that she'd just hang up on me.

So I didn't.

☹☹☹

About ten minutes after that . . .

Dearest Diary,

I was sitting in my bedroom STILL worrying about Zoe when I heard the phone ringing. And then Mum knocking on my door.

Maybe it was Zoe! Calling me!

YESSSS!

I raced out of my room and into the kitchen and picked up the phone.

The Bad News

It wasn't Zoe. ☹

The Good News

It was Peach! ☺

The Even ~~Gooder~~ Better News!

She wants me to come over to her place again tomorrow after school so we can have a go on her new trampoline. And maybe even try some different kinds of flips!

WOO HOO!

Yours 4 ever,

Ella ☺☺☺

Friday afternoon, after school

Dear Diary,

Zoe wasn't on our corner *again* this morning.

And she **still** isn't talking to me.

She even put a wall up on our table, in case I accidentally knock or touch or breathe on any of her things.

Which makes it a teeny-tiny bit hard for her to learn her lines for the TV ad next week.

Especially as there are some new lines to learn! The importerant TV ad people sent them through to Mum last night.

At the **very first starting part** of the ad, we have to jump up onto the trampoline wearing sweet little googy-egg outfits.

And then we both bounce up and down healthily, holding up an egg. (Not the same egg. That would just be weird. And also egg-ceptionally trickerous to do.)

And then I say:

I'm Oogy Googy One!

And Zoe says:

And I'm Oogy Googy Two!

And then we say:

And then we both have to do an egg flip. Still holding onto our eggs!

(Which is going to be exTREMEly trickerous to do, Diary, without smashing them into smithereens if we drop them.)

I hope Zoe starts talking (and listening) to me again soon.

Sorry, Diary. I have to stop writing now so I can get ready to go to Peach's place.

Chat soon.

E

Friday night, very late, in bed

Dearest Diary,

I went to Peach's house! Again!

And it was amazing! And wonderful! And fantabulously fabulous!

The first thing we did was have a go on her trampoline.

Peach showed me how to do some really cool gymnastical moves on it.

Like seat drops.

And pike jumps.

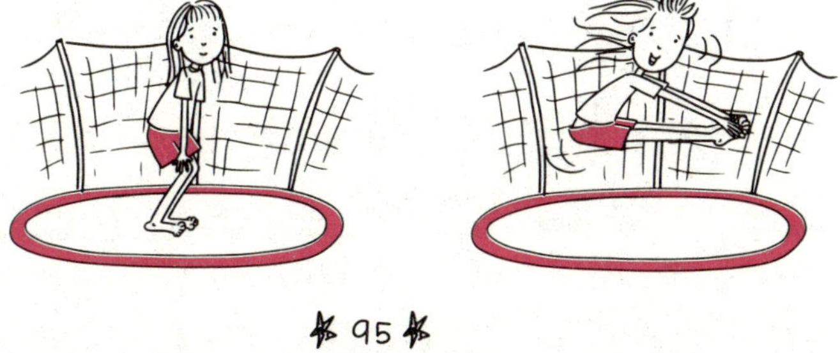

And straddle jumps.

These ones were heaps more fun than when we do them at Twisters, our gymnastics club.

She even showed me a special new way to do a backflip. In case I might ever need to do one on a trampoline for an importerant reason.

I was **SHOCKED!**

How did Peach know that I actually **do** have a **very importerant reason** for knowing how to do a backflip on a trampoline?

It's like she has special MAGICAL ABILITIES! Like that lady who always sits at a little table in a stripy tent at the school fete every year. And tells everyone what their future is going to be.

Peach isn't just aMAZing at predicting the future. She is also super aMAZing at doing gymnastical moves. HEAPS better than Zoe.

Which means she'd be PERFECT for the part of Oogy Googy Two.

Or would she?

Anyway, after a bit more bouncing Peach's mum came out with some cool drinks and mini quiches on a tray.

And guess what Peach told me while we were eating them?

She's going to have a pool party tomorrow! For all her closest friends! With special themed music and food and pool toys!

And she wants me to come to it! As her VSG*! ♥♥♥

*VSG = Very Special Guest

And guess what she told me next? You never will in a pazillion batrillion years, so I'll just tell you.

Peach told me the main reason she wants me to come is because I'm a REALLY FUN person! Much more funnerer than any of her other friends.

And also the nicest, kindest, cleverest person in our class.

And also exCEPTionally talented at all the same things she likes doing. Like dancing. And singing. And actoring. And fashion design.

But **MOST** of all, gymnastical things like front flips and backflips.

And she wishes I could be one of her main friends. Maybe even a BFF, like we used to be back in Grade 3.

ZOW-IE. Hearing all of that felt really weird. But a nice kind of weird. ☺

And we absolutely totally did used to have have lots of fun together.

Have to stop writing now, Diary. I am sooo tired after all that bouncing.

And eating.

And listening.

And thinking.

I will write more tomorrow, I promise!

Yours 4 ever and ever,

Ella

XXX

Saturday night, in bed

Dear Diary,

I practised my lines for the TV ad again this morning.

I was hoping Zoe might call to say she wanted to come over to my place today, so we could practise being Oogy Googies together.

But she didn't. I guess that means she doesn't want to be BFFs with me anymore. Ever.

So I had to be an Oogy Googy ALL BY MYSELF. ☹☹☹

After I'd said 'Eggs are egg-cellent' and 'egg-citing' and 'eggs-hilarating' about 900 times, I was EGGS-HAUSTED.

So I stopped practising my lines in front of the mirror and got ready to go to Peach's pool party instead.

The first thing I did was take all of my summer clothes out of my wardrobe and sort them into piles on my bed.

Then I tried out different outfits, to see which was the most stylish one.

After that I collected all the things I needed to go swimming in Peach's pool.

Then I waited ~~payshently~~ ~~paichently~~ patiently in the lounge room for Dad to be ready so he could drive me over to Peach's house with all my pool stuff.

~~Unforch~~ Unfortunately, Bob chewed up my iced-donut floatie when I wasn't looking.

So I had to borrow Max's *baby* floaties instead.

Bleuchhh.

And guess what? There were hardly any other people at Peach's pool party when I finally got there.

Not even **PEACH'S** **BFFs**, Prinny and Jade!

Just Sharnelle and Chanelle, two girls from the very toppest top class at Twisters. And they were just leaving.

And also Amber-Lee (Peach's cousin) with her mum (Peach's Aunty Mavis), who were visiting from Timbuktooty.

Amber-Lee ate too many mini quiches and got a giganterous stomach-ache and threw up **ALL OVER** Peach's fantabulous flamingo floatie. **Eww.**

So then Peach's aunty and Amber-Lee left too.

And guess what else?

Peach told me Sharnelle and Chanelle had said something **really mean** to Prinny and Jade at Twisters. And that's why Prinny and Jade hadn't come to the party.

And then she started crying. Like this.

Peach was crying so much her face looked **horrendously horrible**. So horrendously horrible I decided to tell her about the importerant TV ad Zoe and I were going to be doing on Monday, in case that cheered her up a bit.

And guess what? It worked!

Peach said **LOVELY THINGS** to me, like how clever I was to get a big part in an importerant ad. On TV! Especially as it was something she'd **ALWAYS** wanted to do herself.

And that she would absolutely, totally, **DEFINITELY** help out if for some reason Zoe (or Ammy) didn't want to be in the ad anymore.

And also how amazingly lucky she was to have a friend she could show how to do perfect flips on a trampoline.

And how now (after all her EXCELLENT coaching) I could do the MOST perfect flips she'd ever seen! HEAPS better than Sharnelle and Chanelle, even though they were in the toppest top class at Twisters.

It made me feel really, really, REALLY special. ☺

Maybe if Zoe doesn't want to be friends anymore, I should ask Peach to be in the importerant TV ad with me instead?

(EsPECially as she's HEAPS better at doing flips than Zoe is.)

Making decisions is **HARD WORK**, Diary. I'm going to have a **BIG THINK** about it all tomorrow.

Good night.

E

Sunday morning

Dear Diary,

I was just doing some more work on my slow loris **Animal Fact File**.

And guess what I found out? Slow lorises might look all fluffy and big-eyed and cute. But they are ~~acksh~~ actually deadly and venomous! As venomous as a deadly snake!

And they keep their venom in a teeny tiny little pocket in the insiderest inside part of their fluffy little arms.

A DEADLY slow loris

A DEADLY snake

Which is just **WEIRD**, Diary. How can something so sweet and cute be so deadly dangerous?

And then there was an **exTREMEly LOUDEROUS** loud knock on my door.

And Olivia barged into my room. AGAIN.

I was just about to tell her to go away (again) when she said Ammy was on the phone.

So I said 'Thank you, darling sister' instead.

And guess what? Ammy said her aunty—the one who is an aMAZingly excellent chef who lives in Paris, France—is staying with her family again.

And she wants me to come over for lunch so I can eat some of her aMAZingly excellent French food.

YES!!! I ♥ French food!

So I said, 'Yes please, what time should I come?'

And Ammy said, 'Come straightaway, right now!'

So I quickly asked Mum if I could go and she (also quickly!) said yes! ☺

Have to go now, Diary! Speak soon!

Love,

Ella

XOXO

Sunday night, after dinner

Dear Diary,

You will never EVER guess who else was at Ammy's house when I got there.

If you said Ammy's amazing French cooking aunty, you are wrong, wrong, WRONG.

It was Zoe.

We were both **SUPER SURPRISED** to see each other.

That's because Ammy didn't tell Zoe that I was going to be there.

And she didn't tell *me* that Zoe was going to be there either.

It was just a **big trickerous trick** to get us in the same room at the same time so we could talk to each other.

This is what we all said next.

Ammy (patiently): Say hello to each other, please.

Zoe (sulkily): Hello.

Me (also sulkily): Hello.

Ammy: Ella, I think Zoe has something she wants to say to you.

Zoe: No I don't.

Ammy: Yes you do. You **TOLD** me you did.

Zoe: OK. How come you went to Peach's pool party yesterday?

How did Zoe even know that? (Unless maybe she's got one of those crystal ball thingies too?)

Me: Because she invited me. How do you know?

Zoe: Because I saw Sharnelle at the library yesterday. And also Chanelle. And THEY told me.

Me: Oh. (Oops.)

Zoe (sulkily): You don't even LIKE Peach.

Me (sulkilier): Well at least she TALKS to me.

And then Zoe said she was sorry about not talking to me. But she was really, really, REALLY confused. And also sad that I'd fibbed to her about Max being sick so I could go to Peach's house instead of rehearsing our lines together.

But mainly because I was spending all my time with a **NEW BEST FRIEND**, instead of with her and Ammy. And now she was worried I didn't want to be her best friend anymore. ☹

Me: Of course you're still my best friend! I'm really, **REALLY** sorry I told you a fib.

Zoe: But why did you go there?

Me: Because she invited me. And I wanted to find out why.

Zoe: Hmmmph.

Me: I'm sorry I hurt your feelings.

Me (again): I just didn't think you'd understand.

Zoe: You didn't even give me a chance to!

Zoe looked all upset again. So Ammy (quickly) asked what I did the first time I went to Peach's house.

I told them about all the fun things we did.

Painting portraits

Choosing fabric for curtains

Eating yummy snacks

Bouncing on her trampoline

Then Zoe said maybe I would want to choose Peach to be in the importerant TV ad now, instead of her.

EsPECially as Peach was probably better at doing flips than she was.

So then I told Zoe I didn't care if Peach was a bazillion patrillion to the power of a kazillion times better at doing flips.

Zoe was my BFFFE. And that counted for EVERYTHING!

So then we did a big giganterous group hug. Like this.

Then we all ran out into Ammy's backyard to have a game of soccer in the sunny sunshine.

It was the besterest, most fantabulous, **most egg-cellent** game of soccer ever!

Yours truly,
Ella
XOXOXO

Monday night

Dearest, darlingest Diary,

We made our importerant TV egg ad today!

Mum drove Zoe and Ammy and me to the **big TV studio** in our car.

We had to get there SUPER early so we could fit in all the things we had to do.

So super early all the birds were still waking up.

First of all Zoe and I practised our lines over and over and OVER again till we got them 100 per cent totally right. Ammy helped.

Then Zoe and I changed into our Oogy Googy outfits and practised a few bounces and egg flips on the trampoline.

Zoe's flips were really good! Almost as good as Peach's.

Then people with giganterous cameras and microphones came out, and a lady with a clipboard said, 'ACTION!'

And we did our healthy egg ad!

Without any mistakes!

Or smashing any of the eggs into smithereens!

We even got our last lines right.

And all the camera people and the lady with the clipboard and Ammy and Mum clapped and cheered!

It was the besterest day of my whole entire life! ☺☺☺

Love,
Ella

A few minutes after that . . .

I forgot to tell you something really importerant!

When we got home from making the ad, Dad told me that Peach had called. And she'd needed to talk to me ~~ERGENTLY~~ URGENTLY straightaway about something!

So I called her back. And guess what Peach wanted to tell me?

She had a BRILLIANT idea for a new super amazing and egg-cellent flip I could do for the TV ad.

And if I came over to her house she would show me how to do it!

So then I said, 'Thanks, but it's too late because Zoe and I already made the importerant TV ad today.'

But I didn't get to tell her what the guess what was, because she hung up on me.

I guess Peach didn't really want to be my friend after all.

Ella

PS A few weeks later

Our healthy egg ad came on TV!

And everyone* at school (even kids we'd never even met before) kept coming up to us and saying things like, 'So get cracking!' and 'Get into eggs!'

* Except for Princess Peach. And her friends Prinny and Jade.

Hehehe. Making TV ads is aMAZing. And FABulous. And EGG-cellently EGG-cellent!

PPS A few days after that

Mum told me the importerant TV ad people called her.

On the phone!

And they said they were so impressed with our actoring skills they want us to make **another** TV ad very soon!

And this time they want **THREE** kids to be in the ad.

Which means Ammy can be in it as well!

☺☺☺

I wonder what it's going to be about?

Ella Diaries

Read more of Ella's brilliant diary in

Double Dare You

Ballet Backflip

I ♥ Pets

Dreams come true

Christmas Chaos

Pony School Showdown

Friends Not Forever

Worst Camp Ever

Operation Merry Christmas

Friendship S.O.S

Going Green

Total TV Drama

Goal Power

Diary Disaster

The Super Secret Club

Gym Squad Tumble

Time to Shine

Wildlife Rescue!

Passion for Fashion

Christmas Crackers

and look out for more coming soon!